The Rescue Dogs

by Jessica Quilty

Scott Foresman
is an imprint of

Glenview, Illinois • Boston, Massachusetts • Chandler, Arizona
Upper Saddle River, New Jersey

ISBN 13: 978-0-328-50816-7
ISBN 10:   0-328-50816-0

6 7 8 9 10 V010 15 14 13 12

This dog helps find people lost in the mountains.

Rescue workers help people. Sometimes dogs help rescue workers.

Some rescue dogs
help the police.

Rescue dogs can find people who are lost. They can pull people away from danger.

4

A dog's sense of smell is very strong. Rescue dogs use it to find missing people.

Some rescue dogs live with families. A family gets a dog when it is a puppy. They teach it many things.

The dog learns to listen. Once it has heard an order, the dog must act! It must not break the rules. When the dog is ready, it can go to work.

Rescue dogs have happy and busy lives. Maybe one will help you someday!